I Swim an Ocean in My Sleep

NORMA FARBER

ILLUSTRATED BY ELIVIA SAVADIER

HENRY HOLT AND COMPANY

NEW YORK

For Daniel and Sadye and the sea
For Stanley and our dreams
whatever they may be
—E. S.

Henry Holt and Company, Inc.
Publishers since 1866
115 West 18th Street
New York, New York 10011

Henry Holt is a registered trademark of Henry Holt and Company, Inc.

Published in Canada by Fitzhenry & Whiteside Ltd.,
195 Allstate Parkway, Markham, Ontario L3R 4T8.

Library of Congress Cataloging-in-Publication Data
Farber, Norma. I swim an ocean in my sleep / Norma Farber; illustrated by Elivia Savadier.
Summary: A dream takes the reader into the ocean world with its
coral castle fairyland, schools of swimmers, dancing lobsters, and
other creatures of the deep.
[1. Dreams—Fiction.   2. Ocean—Fiction.   3. Stories in rhyme.]
I. Savadier, Elivia, ill.   II. Title.
PZ8.3.F224Iaah   1996   [E]—dc20   95-25689

ISBN 0-8050-3381-5
First Edition—1997
Printed in the United States of America on acid-free paper.∞

1   3   5   7   9   10   8   6   4   2

The artist used ink and gouache on vinyl-coated
cotton window-shade material to create
the illustrations for this book.

Night is dark,
night is deep.

I swim an ocean in my sleep.

Night is filmy,
night is far.
I dream upon an ocean star.

Star five-fingered,
starry fish,
let me dream my favorite wish.

Foam be pillow
for my head,
ocean billow be my bed.

Coral, climb
from bottom sand
into castled fairyland.

Friends be fishes
by my side,
schools of swimmers in the tide.

Fins, row on
in double file.

Night, stretch out and stay a while.

Boats, flow over
friends and me
jumping rope in weeds of sea.

Whale, approach
and let me ride
now atop and now inside.

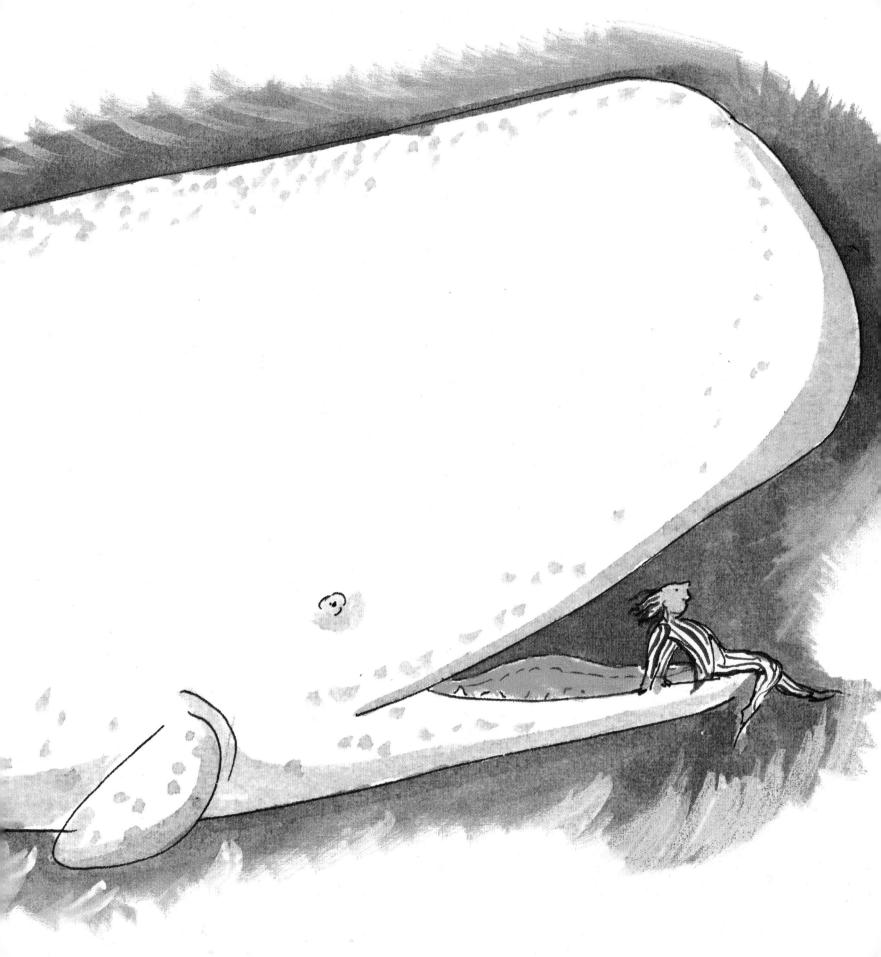

Lobster, dance
into my net.
Clam, click-click your castanet.

Oyster, open!
Pearl, come here!
Let me wear you in my ear.

Ocean deep,
ocean dim,
fill my dreaming to the brim.

Night's so long,
the dark will last
if I do not dream too fast.

Hello, mermaid
in a wave
streaming upward from your cave!

Dream is dark, dream is deep,
I swim an ocean in my sleep.

Seas may never
wash away
if I never dream of day.

But I'm dreaming
sun and noon
and a blazing red balloon.

Now good-bye
to fish and foam,
for it's time to paddle home.

Dreaming deep,
sleeping tight,
I swam a slumber sea of night.

Now it's time
to step once more

wakened on a morning shore.